Contents

INTRODUCTION

Your home is one of the most expensive things you'll ever pay for, so whether you're renting or buying, you should take good care of it. While you'll probably be tempted to call a professional when something breaks, you can take care of a lot of problems yourself.

Most of these home repairs can be done with little to no experience. However, always be sure to do research on anything you don't understand, particularly if you're dealing with electricity, which can be extremely hazardous. Also, if you don't already have a tool kit of your own, this wouldn't be a bad time to start building your essential toolbox. Some of the repairs listed here will require special tools you may not have laying around, but we'll list those where applicable.

A broken toilet lever is pretty easy to fix. In most cases, if pressing the lever doesn't flush the toilet, you can just pop the tank open and re-attach the chain. However, in some cases, the handle itself can become corroded or any one of the pieces that connect the handle to the flapper (including the handle, nut, metal rod, or chain) can break. All of these parts can be replaced on the cheap, though.

The garbage disposal is a big scary machine made of hidden blades and bad noises. However, primal fears of ominous pits aside, it's actually fairly easy to clear up a clog. You'll need to cut the power to the unit to prevent any accidents. Some units are plugged into an outlet in your cabinet, but others may be wired directly to the wall. Once the disposal is disabled, you can use an allen wrench to adjust the flywheel inside the disposal. Do this by placing the allen wrench in the hole in the center of the bottom of the unit.

Holes in walls are nearly unavoidable, even if you're only renting. However, unless you've done plowed a car through it, you can fix most holes pretty cheaply. The simplest holes to fix are going to be screw or nail holes from hanging everything from pictures to TVs. For holes like these, you'll want to clean the area of any debris and wipe down the wall. Use a putty knife to press some spackle into the wall and let it dry.

CHAPTER ONE

A home is a living space used as a permanent or semi-permanent residence for an individual, family, household or several families in a tribe. It is often a house, apartment, or other building, or alternatively a mobile home, houseboat, yurt or any other portable shelter.

Most Popular House Styles

Do you know your favorite house style? To answer that question, you'll need to be well versed in the most popular architecture styles in America. These house styles have made up the landscape of suburbs and cities for the last couple hundred years.

Once you know your style, you'll be able to envision your perfect dream home. You can either buy an old home or build a house in your favorite style from the ground up. If you want a newly built home that incorporates a past house style, learn about some of the key characteristics that make each home stand apart.

Cape Cod

Cape cod homes are extremely common in suburban communities and became increasingly popular in the United States during the 1950s. The style was originally introduced by English settlers in the late 17th century and is named after the coast of Massachusetts. These homes tend to be a story and a half and include dormers and a central doorway. The original design was inspired by English half-timbered houses from centuries prior, but the frame was altered to suit the New England climate.

Victorian

Victorian architecture refers to an era of design instead of one specific style. Victorian homes were built from the early 1800s through the early 1900s during the reign of Queen Victoria. Since the era is generally associated with a rising middle class and increasing wealth, these homes tend to be larger and more elaborate. Victorian architecture was influenced by several prolific architects and varying cityscapes.

Some variations of a Victorian-style home include:

o Queen Anne

o Italianate

o Eastlake

o Romanesque Revival

o Gothic Revival

Colonial

Colonial style homes date back to the 17th century, and the homes come in many variations. Each style was influenced by early American settlers depending on their country of origin, and the homes usually feature symmetry and some type of dormer. More commonly, you'll see examples of British or Georgian colonial-style homes since a large portion of America was under British rule early on.

You might also find these colonial styles:

o Federal Colonial

o Dutch Colonial

o French Colonial

o Spanish Colonial

Craftsman

The craftsman style home came about in the early 20th century during the Arts and Crafts movement. These homes put a particular focus on materials and motifs that are inspired by nature. You'll commonly find naturally toned woodwork, geometric stained glass, and several built-ins. The color palette of craftsman-style home tends to be earthy in nature and include shades like forest green, rusty orange, and natural browns.

Some of the common variations of the craftsman style include:

o Mission

o Bungalow

o Stickley

Prairie

This style of home was first crafted by an innovative turn of the century architect, Frank Lloyd Wright. Homes are inspired by their relationship to nature and feature lots of handcrafted details like simple woodwork, stained glass, and built-in furniture. This style of home was heavily influenced by the Arts and

Crafts movement, but it is distinct from craftsman-style homes. Only a handful of original homes exist, but the style is still an iconic example of architecture that originated in America.

Ranch

Ranch homes are single-story or split level houses that started popping up in the United States during the first half of the 20th century. In the 1930s, people built these homes that were inspired by Spanish colonials in the Southwest. Later examples of these homes can sometimes be confused with mid-Century modern homes because they share some characteristics. In general, ranch style homes have open floor plans and connect to the outside.

Tudor

Tudor style homes are easily recognizable and are inspired by historical homes in England. This home style became popular in the early 20th century in wealthy suburban communities. You'll also find newer subdivisions using this style on homes built within the last forty years.

Mediterranean

This popular American home style was influenced by homes in the Mediterranean and became popular in the Southern United States in the early 1900s. Homes often feature warm tones, stucco exteriors, and beautiful ornamental details incorporated into the tile and woodwork.

Modern

It's easy to confuse modern homes with contemporary ones, but the easiest way to tell the difference is to look at who built the home and when. Mid century modern homes were built around the 1940s through the 1970s. In contrast, contemporary homes weren't built until decades later. Modern homes are generally minimal in style and have simple, geometric lines.

Contemporary

As you learned above, modern architecture was built in the middle of the 20th century whereas contemporary homes are still being built today. Contemporary homes can vary greatly, but they tend to fuse the interior design with the exterior design so there is a sense of flow. While the style can be minimal, edges could be soft and rounded.

Farmhouse

A farmhouse-style home is a modern interpretation of a home that is situated on plenty of acreage. These homes have been built for centuries and typically serve to help families live off the land, so to speak. Old farmhouses come in various other design styles, like Victorian or Colonial. However, many farmhouses were built with simple details in a more vernacular style.

Cottage

Modest cottage-style homes originated in Europe and are part of the vernacular architecture of several small towns and villages. Cottages are defined by their small size and are usually faced with stone or wood. Most of these homes are found in rural communities and have an old-world charm.

Cabin

Small log cabins have been built by locals for several hundred years. This primitive style of building originally consisted of modest one-room homes in the woods. Nowadays, people build modern cabins as their primary residence in rural and even suburban settings for the aesthetic.

Row House

Rowhouses, also known as townhouses, are homes that are built directly next to one another. This type of house is common in cities like Brooklyn and Philadelphia, where lot sizes are tiny and narrow. These homes were generally built by a sole architect for working-class families. Modern-day townhouses will have the same space-saving qualities but more modern features.

Greek Revival

Greek Revival and other classical architecture in America is inspired by buildings from ancient Greece and Rome. You can find several old Greek

Revivial homes and buildings that feature large columns, stucco exteriors, and classical order details.

Top Architectural Styles

The built environment is a rich and varied architectural tapestry with overlapping styles and movements that have often traveled around the world, adapting themselves to different climates, landscapes and cultural needs. Here is a rundown of 15 popular architectural styles throughout history.

Classical Architecture

An umbrella term that refers to the building styles that originated in ancient Greece and Rome, classical architecture has influenced centuries of subsequent design movements throughout the world, including Neoclassical and Greek Revival architecture. Some of the most famous buildings in the modern world are based on ancient Greek and Roman designs. Classical architecture focuses on symmetry and proportions; columns with Doric, Ionic, or Corinthian detailing; the use of materials such as marble, brick, and concrete; and classical design motifs such as interior molding, medium pitched roofs, boxed eaves, decorative door surrounds, and broken pediments over the entry door.

While classical architecture was largely replaced by modernism and contemporary architecture in the 20th century, classical architecture continues to be built in what has been rebranded as "new classical" style.

Neoclassical Architecture

Neoclassical architecture refers to a style of buildings constructed during the revival of Classical Greek and Roman architecture that began around 1750 and flourished in the 18th and 19th centuries. Whereas Greek Revival architecture utilizes classical elements, such as columns with Doric, Ionic, or Corinthian details, neoclassicism is characterized by a more whole-scale revival of entire and often grand-scale classical volumes.

Some of the most famous and easily recognizable institutional and government buildings in Europe and the United States are neoclassical in style, such as the White House and U.S. Capitol building.

Greek Revival Architecture

Greek Revival architecture is inspired by the symmetry, proportion, simplicity, and elegance of the ancient Greek temples of 5th century B.C. In the U.S., Greek Revival reached peak popularity from 1825 to 1860, and became the first dominant national style of architecture in the U.S. as it spread from the East Coast across the country to the West Coast, leaving state capitol buildings, banks, New England churches, urban row houses, galleried cottages, and southern plantation houses in its wake.

Inspired by the birthplace of democracy, Americans borrowed classical elements to design buildings for what was then a still new democracy, such as columns with Doric, Ionic, or Corinthian details, painted white to mimic the marble used in ancient Greece; gently sloping roofs with gable fronts; and elaborate door surrounds. Interiors featured simple, fairly open layouts; graceful proportions; tall parlor floor windows and doors; ornate plasterwork ceilings; plain plaster walls; wide plank floors; and ornate ceiling mantels.

Industrial Architecture

An umbrella term used to describe buildings constructed to facilitate the needs of industry, industrial architecture encompasses a range of building types and styles that mix functionality and design and can be found all over the industrialized world, such as factories, warehouses, foundries, steel mills, water towers, grain silos, distilleries, breweries, refineries, power plants, and other utilitarian structures. The first industrial buildings were constructed in the 1700s during the first Industrial Revolution that took place mainly in Britain from 1760 to 1830.

But today when we reference industrial architecture, we are mostly referring to the buildings that emerged as a response to the widespread use of new materials such as metal and concrete as well as mass production methods brought on by the Second Industrial Revolution of the late 19th and early 20th century, and which formed the building blocks for Modern Architecture. Features of industrial architecture may include large, open floor plans; high ceilings; raw rough materials such as concrete, brick, and metal; lack of ornamentation on building façade; exposed brick, ductwork and piping; and large metal-grid windows.

Bauhaus Architecture

Bauhaus architecture came out of the influential German school founded by Walter Gropius (1883-1969) in the early 20th century, which had a utopian aim to create a radically new form of architecture and design to help rebuild society after World War I. By synthesizing fine arts, crafts, design, architecture, and technology, the Bauhaus promoted rational, functional design that embraced a form follows function, less is more ethos.

Not all Bauhaus buildings look alike, but in general they eschew ornamentation to focus on simple, rational, functional design; use simple geometric forms such as the triangle, square, and circle; asymmetry; use of modern materials such as steel, glass, concrete; flat roofs; glass curtain walls; smooth façades. Bauhaus developed into the International Style when Gropius and other prominent members of the Bauhaus emigrated to the

U.S. in the 1930s and later influenced the development of modernism in the 1950s and '60s. Bauhaus architecture and design principles still influence the shape and look of everyday objects.

Victorian Architecture

The term Victorian architecture refers not to a particular style but to an era—the reign of Queen Victoria from 1837 to 1901. The style originated in England and still largely defines the architecture of its cities and towns, but varying styles of Victorian era architecture spread to places like North America, Australia, and New Zealand. Victorian era architecture is marked by its unapologetic devotion to ornament and its ornate interior design. Some features that will help you spot a Victorian from the outside include: steeply pitched roofs; plain or colorfully painted brick; ornate gables; rooftop finials; sliding sash and bay windows; octagonal or round towers; and generous wraparound porches. Interiors often include grand staircases; complicated layouts; high ceilings; intricately carved wood paneling; and decorative fireplaces.

The Arts and Crafts movement was a reaction to the ornate and mass produced styles of Victorian architecture that embraced handcrafted design and the use of natural materials such as stone, brick, wood, and hammered copper and bronze metalwork detailing. Originating in Great Britain in the mid 19th-century, the Arts and Crafts movement migrated to the U.S. in the beginning of the 20th century, encompassing architecture, interior design, textiles, fine art and more. Many architectural styles came out of the Arts and Crafts movement, including the popular Craftsman and Bungalow-style homes, simple, thoughtfully made structures originally designed for working class families.

Arts and Crafts-style homes are symmetrical; low to the ground; designed for efficiency and minimal upkeep; often feature large fireplaces; low-pitched roofs with wide overhangs; exposed interior beams; built-in bookshelves, window seats and cabinets; and multiple windows with small panes; prominent porches; and open floor plans.

Cape Cod Architecture

Cape Cod architecture is named after the Massachusetts coastal region where it is the signature style. Homey and effortlessly appealing, Cape Cod houses have simple, timeless clean-lined silhouettes, with elements such as oak and pine wood post and beam framing and wood flooring; brick fireplaces; and clapboard or cedar shake roof and side shingles. English colonists in the 17th century first adapted English half-timber hall and parlor houses to suit the bitter New England climate, creating a boxier, lower slung silhouette to stand up to the elements. A second wave known as Cape Cod Revival in the 1920s to the 1950s helped popularize the style, which spread across the United States, and became an economical solution during both the Depression and the post-war housing boom of the 1940s and '50s. Even in super-sized 21st-century America, Cape Cod style homes retain a nostalgic popular appeal with new builds of all sizes today, from sprawling homes to tiny houses.

Tudor Architecture

Originating in England during the Tudor period starting in 1485, Tudor architecture evokes storybook cottages and old world charm. Tudor homes were built by craftsmen who combined Renaissance and Gothic design elements to create a transitional style that spread throughout England until it was supplanted by Elizabethan architecture in 1558. Tudor style was reborn in the United States in the 1890s and remained popular through the 1940s. Tudor homes feature signature half-timber detailing, long vertically placed decorative wood beams that create a two-toned exterior. However, Tudor Revival homes often eschewed this original Tudor look for red-toned brick with ornate detailing around windows, chimneys, and entryways.

Art Deco Architecture

Art Deco architecture is part of the Art Deco movement, an inventive design period in the U.S. and Europe in the 1920s and 30s that spanned the realms of fashion, art, homewares, and building styles throughout the Roaring Twenties and the Great

Depression. The earliest examples of Art Deco architecture can be found in Paris, France, before the style spread to the United States in the 1930s, influencing the skyline of Manhattan forever with now iconic skyscrapers such as the Empire State Building, Rockefeller Center, and the Chrysler building.

Art Deco buildings utilize materials like stucco, terracotta, decorative glass, chrome, steel, and aluminum. They feature ornate, geometric detailing such as chevrons, pyramids, stylized sunbursts or florals, zig-zags, and other geometric shapes. Many Art Deco buildings feature bright, opulent colors accented with contrasting black, white, gold or silver. And they often feature fragmented triangular shapes; decorative, geometric windows; parapets and spires.

Modern Architecture

Modern architecture refers to the style of architecture that flourished in the early to mid 20th century. Rejecting the ornamental styles of the recent past, modern architecture favors clean lines; functional design; open floor plans; built-in storage; a focus on materials such as steel, concrete, iron, glass, wood, brick, and stone; and a focus on integrating architecture into the natural landscape while bringing the outdoors inside with the use of large windows to let in natural light and air.

Modern architects such as Frank Lloyd Wright redefined a new world of architecture with form follows function design, and a host of mid-century designers transformed the built landscape and the world of interior design with mid-century modern furniture that continues to be wildly popular today.

Brutalist Architecture

Brutalist architecture (1950s-1970s) is characterized by simple, block-like, hulking concrete structures (the term is a play on the French phrase for raw concrete, béton brut). With simple, graphic lines, a heavy appearance, a monochromatic palette, and a lack of ornamentation, Brutalism is a bold, in-your-face and eternally polarizing style. An offshoot of modernism, brutalist architecture became a popular if perennially controversial choice for institutional buildings around the world before fading out in the 1980s, giving way to the postmodernism and today's contemporary styles. But the style's influence can be seen in contemporary product and interior design, furniture, objects, and web design.

Contemporary Architecture
Contemporary architecture is a blanket phrase that comprises a range of present day building styles that often look radically different from one another and sometimes from anything that has come before. Contemporary architecture followed the modern period of the first half of the 20th century and the postmodern period through the 90s. Using innovative materials and building methods such as computer-generated curves, laser-cutting technology, and 3D printing, contemporary architects often embrace rounded forms, curved lines, unconventional volumes, asymmetry, and open floor plans. Sustainability is an important feature of contemporary architecture.

Beaux-Arts Architecture

Beaux-Arts architecture is a building style that emerged from Paris' École des Beaux-Arts in the late 1800s and spread to the US during the Gilded Age. Beaux-Arts buildings are grandiose, theatrical, highly ornate buildings that are inspired by Roman and Greek classicism and inspired by French and Italian Renaissance and Baroque building styles, such as the Musée D'Orsay.

Notable American architects such as Richard Morris, HH Richardson and Charles McKim trained at the Beaux-Arts school in Paris, and Beaux-Arts style was embraced for major building projects in the US, such as the Library of Congress in Washington D.C. and prominent buildings such as Grand Central Terminal and the New York Public Library's main branch in NYC. Beaux-Arts architecture faded around 1930 with the onset of the Depression rendering such over-the-top displays of opulence as out of touch and obsolete.

Italianate architecture refers to a particular 19th-century style of building that was inspired by 16th century Italian Renaissance architecture combined with picturesque influences that featured architectural elements from a romanticized past that broke some of the strict rules around formal

The Italianate style was born in 1802 when architect John Nash built the first Italianate villa in England, Cronkhill in Shropshire, and was promoted by the work of Sir Charles Barry in the 1830s. The style spread throughout Northern Europe, the British Empire and the US from the late 1840s to 1890. It was a hugely popular building choice used in both rural and urban settings in the US in the 1860s after the Civil War.

The House Hunt

At each step of the home buying process, from browsing to buying and from measuring the markets to managing your mortgage, preparation is as essential as flexibility, creativity and imagination.

Be A Better Browser

When you're ready to make the dream of a new home a reality, where do you begin? As with nearly any endeavor, your house hunt may very well begin online. With dozens of reputable real estate sites to choose from, it's easy to while away the hours (days, weeks and even months!) browsing for homes. But, where, when and for how much? Every fruitful search begins with both a specific goal and a flexible approach. Know what you're looking for: Is it a sense of the market or a specific home? If you think you know where you want to live but can't find any listings you like, check out surrounding areas. Beyond listing prices, be sure to pay attention to market trends, municipal services, crime rates, school ratings (which affect home values whether or not you have a family) as well as property taxes, which can make a big difference in carry costs as well as resale value.

Take The Long View

As you start looking at homes in person, try to visualize the potential in each home, both upside and downside. First impressions can be deceiving. Though you may fall in love at first sight, this is not always a sign that a house is destined to be your dream home. Likewise, a less-than-perfect house in a great location can be customized to suit your style. A charming fixer-upper may require more of an investment than you can make. A larger home, while allowing room to grow, may take a lot of work to maintain. Go too small and you may be looking for a new home sooner than you'd like. Moving is not only a lot of work, but it's also expensive. As you house hunt, look at least 5 years into the future. Your future self will thank you!

Measure The Markets

If you have some flexibility in terms of either geography or time, it's always best to look in a buyer's market: one where the economics, inventory and pricing trends make buying most attractive and affordable. How can you tell if it's a buyer or seller's market? A buyer's market occurs when the supply (available properties for sale) exceeds demand (the number of buyers seeking to purchase properties). In a buyer's market, you may be able to buy a great home for a lower cost than you would in a seller's market. A seller's market occurs when demand exceeds supply, or there are more buyers seeking to purchase properties than there are available homes on the market. If you're buying a home in a seller's market, be aware that sellers have the advantage. Trying to get a lower sale price probably won't work to your advantage. In fact, you could lose the opportunity to purchase the property altogether if a competing buyer makes a higher offer. This is where your trusted real estate agent is perhaps most helpful. They will compare sales data and other local property values to help you make a reasonable offer. Your agent will also draw up an offer letter and submit it to the seller or the seller's representative.

In a buyer's market, you have more flexibility to include some contingencies in your offer. Inspection contingencies are pretty standard. If the inspection on the house reveals that repairs are needed, the purchase price you've offered is subject to change. If your agent feels the market conditions are truly in your favor, you may also request some upgrades in your offer as well as additional items, like furnishings.

In a seller's market, you'll have less leeway with contingencies. Again, trust your real estate agent on this. Also bear in mind that your offer will include what's called an earnest money deposit, which is essentially a small advance you make toward your down payment to the seller. Your earnest money deposit is usually equal to 1% – 3% of the purchase price of your home. Be 100% sure you want to purchase a home before you submit an offer because, if you back out, you may lose your deposit.

Be Ready To Buy

When the home you want appears, you need to be ready to make an offer on the spot. So once you decide you're serious about buying (maybe even before you begin browsing) you'll want to have a downpayment ready and preapproval on a mortgage. You'll need to have a budget set, considering your total income, debt, monthly expenses and how much you can comfortably afford for a down payment. This will give you a better sense of what's realistic in terms of a purchase price and how much and what type of mortgage may work best for you. Having a mortgage preapproval gives you a good idea of how much house you can afford, your interest rate and the types of loan programs you qualify for. A mortgage preapproval also tells sellers and real estate agents that you won't have trouble finding funding for your home purchase. This gives your eventual home offer more weight.

Keep in mind that a preapproval is different from a prequalification. When you get prequalified for a loan, your lender doesn't verify the claims you make about your credit and income. On the other hand, a preapproval requires a credit check and sometimes underwriting. A prequalification holds less weight than a preapproval because it often doesn't include those details. When you get a preapproval, you get the most accurate information possible about how much of a loan you can obtain. This benefits everyone involved with your home search.

When you better understand the home-buying process, finding the perfect home can be a little easier and less stressful. Look for a mortgage lender who's responsive to your questions and offers an easy way to apply for a mortgage, like Rocket Mortgage® by Quicken Loans®. A preapproval from Rocket Mortgage® offers a quick application process and preapproval online. With their industry leading technology and tools, Rocket Mortgage created a better home buying experience centered around you – personalized, convenient and clear. So you can focus on making your house, home.

CHAPTER TWO

How to Renovate a House

Judging by shows on DIY Network and HGTV, it takes approximately 24 minutes to renovate a house. Everyone knows this is not true, but this style of fast-shot remodeling presided over by glib hosts takes away from the core notion that home renovation is complex and difficult. A look at the major elements of a whole-house renovation will give you a sense of what's involved.

1. Design and Planning

A sketch on a cocktail napkin, full-blown architectural plans, or just a firm set of thoughts about how the remodel should progress. It is cheaper and less frustrating to correct mistakes before the remodel takes physical form. Ensure that you have funding for your renovation.

• Draw up a simple "yes/no" list of do-it-yourself projects and projects you want professionals to do.

• Look for contractors and subcontractors for those jobs you do not want to do yourself.

• Apply for permits.

2. Roof, Foundation, Water Issues, Siding, Windows

Roof replacement or repair; foundation fix; stopping water infiltration; installing or repairing siding and windows. Large projects must be done first because subsequent projects are impacted by them.

• Protect your future renovation work by making certain the house won't collapse on you (foundation, major structural problems) and that it will remain dry (roof, siding, windows).

• Secure the foundation.

• Make major foundation repairs to areas such as weakened walls, joists, and carrying beams.

• Repair or replace the roof.

• Replace seriously damaged windows that may threaten future remodeling work. If not seriously damaged, leave it for later in the process.

• If the siding is so damaged that it will allow water infiltration, repair or replace the siding. If not seriously damaged, leave it for later in the process.

3. Demolition

Demolishing and disposing of sections of the house that will be replaced by later projects.

• Rent a large container for waste.

• Carefully demolish all or some of the areas of the house that will be renovated. Demolish as much as possible if you will not be living in the house.

• Exercise caution when demolishing surfaces coated with lead-based paint.

4. Structural Carpentry

Carpentry that is in support of other work such as drywall, new or moved walls, windows, doors, etc.

• Moving walls.

• Constructing new walls.

• Adding beams to support a greater weight upstairs.

• Punching in new doors (or removing existing doors).

• Adding framing for new construction windows, or significantly enlarging the window openings.

5. HVAC Ductwork, Electrical, and Plumbing

Vital services that need to be installed when the walls and ceiling are open.

• With the walls and ceiling open, it is time for the HVAC company to install ductwork for central heating and air conditioning.

• Run new electrical and plumbing systems. Electrical and plumbing inspectors will visit at this time, too.

6. Windows

Installing new-construction or replacement windows.

• Window installation, whether whole-house or partial, almost always plays into a home remodel project.

7. Insulation

Laying the insulation in the walls and ceiling.

• Install insulation in the walls and attic.

• Insulation goes fast, so make sure that your drywall company is ready to go soon after this.

8. Drywall

Closing up the walls with drywall: hanging it, mudding it, and sanding it.

• A second inspection from the electrical inspector (and perhaps the plumbing inspector) will give you the go-ahead to close up the walls.

• Drywallers hang sheets of drywall, apply drywall compound, and let the compound dry. After drying, they sand it smooth. Sometimes, they will repeat the process until they achieve a seamless surface.

9. Fine Carpentry

Carpentry that is not supportive: baseboards, molding, trim around windows and doors, built-in elements (bookcases, breakfast nooks, etc.).

• Fine carpenters give your house that finished touch.

10. Interior Painting, Wallpaper, and Other Surface Finishes

Painting interior walls, hanging wallpaper, painting molding and trim, staining and sealing trim.

• All of these detail-oriented surface finishes should be one of the last items you do indoors as this work can damage other work of yours.

• Should you paint before installing or sanding your flooring or the reverse? This is debatable. Laying flooring first means that paint might get on the flooring. Painting first means that the floor sander may scuff your walls.

11. Flooring

Your final floor covering—laminate, solid hardwood, tile, engineered wood.

• Installing the flooring as late as possible in the renovation process saves your flooring surface from significant damage.

12. Siding, Gutters

Exterior work on the outside of the house.

• With the house mostly finished, it is safe to put on the siding. You do not want to do this earlier (unless absolutely necessary) because doors and windows may get punched out, ruining the siding.

13. Major Auxiliary Building

Any buildings that are detached from the main house.

• Additions
• Sunrooms
• Swimming pools

Home Repair Skill Levels Explained

Doing your own home repairs can be satisfying, creative, and fun. With the right set of home do-it-yourself skills, you can save a considerable amount of money and time. Vital to successful home repairs is the ability to accurately gauge the difficulty of the project in relation to your own home repair skill level, whether beginner, intermediate, or expert.

Safety is at the heart of this. Pushing your limits may seem like a good idea at first, but you may find yourself in over your head. Never hesitate to stop work on any project that feels uncomfortable to you, and to call in a professional to complete the work.

Beginner Home Repair Skill Level

Beginner-level home repairs require few, if any, prior skills before you start. Beginner repairs use common, inexpensive hand tools that many homeowners already own such as hammers and hand saws, along with a limited number of corded or cordless electric tools. Beginner projects usually can be completed within a day, and sometimes within just an hour or two.

Precursor Knowledge

As a beginner, you might be starting with no skill base at all. Generally, though, you already possess skills such as sawing wood by hand, using a cordless drill, painting both with a roller and with a brush, and hammering a nail by hand. Beginner level repairs are not overly physically taxing, with a personal lift maximum requirement of around 50 pounds being the norm.

Beginner Skills vs. Other Skill Levels

As a person with beginner home repair skills, you might have just bought your first home. You may not have had prior opportunities to hone your repair skills. Or you might be a long-time homeowner who, because of extenuating circumstances, has decided to take on more repairs by yourself. Intermediate- and expert-level projects such as building a deck or removing a load-bearing wall might feel daunting, but you are curious and have a willingness to learn new skills. While safety should always be foremost in mind, you can rest easier since beginner level repairs tend to remain more on the safer side than do intermediate or expert level repairs.

Examples of Beginner Home Projects

• Interior painting

• Patching holes in drywall

• Changing a ceiling light

• Fixing concrete patio cracks

• Fixing nail pops in drywall

• Fixing a sticking door

• Relighting a pilot light

• Planning a bathroom layout

• Replacing a bathroom fan grille

Intermediate Home Repair Skill Level

Intermediate level home repair skills are characterized as skills that straddle a fine line between beginner and expert, with ever-changing factors such as timing, budget, physical strength, or the ability to round up assistants tipping the scale in either direction. Intermediate-level repairs can include some permitted work. Repairs at this level often extend for days or weeks. If niche or special tools are required, they are usually low cost and easy to obtain. Often, it can be difficult to distinguish between intermediate and expert projects, especially since intermediate-level homeowners may want to push their skill level a bit further to save money.

Precursor Knowledge

Intermediate home repair skills encompass the entire set of beginner skills, adding experience with a wide range of electric power tools. You may also have an introductory knowledge of dealing with electrical and plumbing systems. This skill level can include tasks that require lifting more than 50 pounds, especially for long periods of time.

Intermediate Skills vs. Other Skill Levels

As a person with intermediate home repair skills, basic repair skills are already second nature to you. You have a full range of hand tools and you are building up a good set of quality power tools. You're willing and anxious to take on more ambitious projects that extend into the expert level. Safety is important to you, and you are careful to employ strict safety practices at all times.

Examples of Intermediate Home Projects

• Exterior painting

• Floor sanding

• Toilet replacement

• Replacing an electrical outlet

• Building a floating, ground-level deck

• Building a retaining wall

• Refinishing a hardwood floor

• Installing a new circuit breaker

Expert Home Repair Skill Level

The expert home repair skill level is one that encompasses nearly the entire gamut of home repair skills. Many of the projects at this level are also performed by certified or licensed professionals such as electricians and plumbers. Codes, permits, and zoning are often involved. Many of these projects require expensive, specialized tools that have limited utility with other projects such as wet tile saws or PEX crimpers. Expert-level skills often touch upon dangerous projects, such as running new circuits out of electric service panels. Projects at this level often can extend into weeks or months.

Precursor Knowledge

As an expert-level do-it-yourselfer, you have experience with most tasks at the beginner and intermediate levels. You know how to use nearly every common electric power tool, plus specialized tools such as electric nailers, powder-actuated nailers, and rotary levels.

Expert Skills vs. Other Skill Levels

You may have already owned a home and this home is your second or third remodel. You might be interested in purchasing and flipping homes for profit. You have done home repairs and improvements for years rather than for months, and you have remodeled entire rooms by yourself or with a partner, allowing you to experience a diverse range of home repairing and remodeling skills. Scale can often define the expert skill level. If replacing a toilet is at the intermediate level, then replacing a toilet plus a myriad of other difficult tasks that constitute an entire bathroom remodel represent the expert level.

Examples of Expert Home Projects

• Bathroom remodeling

• Kitchen remodeling

• Building a raised deck

• Roof replacement

• Water heater replacement

• Removing a load-bearing wall

Licensed Contractors and Specialty Tradespeople

In most jurisdictions, licensing is required for general contractors and tradespeople who deal with electrical, HVAC, and plumbing systems. Often, separate registrations or certifications are needed for specialty contract work like asbestos and lead-based paint removal, demolition and salvage, mold remediation, fireproofing, and landscaping.

As a do-it-yourselfer with beginner and intermediate repair skills, licensed professionals are valuable and necessary for completing home projects effectively and safely. Even do-it-yourselfers at the expert level who are adept at certain skills often hire professionals to perform those same tasks in order to save time.

Hiring and Managing Your Home Repair Contractor

Your "do-it-yourself" attitude is commendable, but at some point, you'll need to hire a home repair contractor and pay someone to fix something in your home. There are going to be situations when you don't have the time, inclination or skill to make a particular repair or do some of the work you need to be done. We all hire someone to fix something in our house at some point. What you'll find here is some guidance on when and how to select a home repair or maintenance contractor.

Types of Home Repair Contractors

When you need repair work done on your home, you will usually hire a specialty type of tradesman called a "subcontractor" which is different than a general contractor (GC) or builder. A general contractor or builder is a company that will construct a major renovation project or build a new home and hires all the individual specialty subcontractors.

The GC is the overall coordinator of a larger project and typically does not provide the labor to build the house. That comes from the subcontractors or the "trades" (construction trades). On a new home or large home repair or renovation project, these subs may include the excavator, concrete sub, rough framing carpentry crew, roofer, plumber, mechanical (HVAC) electrician, finish carpenter, painter, flooring, etc. The GC hires these subcontractors directly and directly "holds" their contracts. That means they work for him and they are under contract to him. You would have a contract with only the GC, not the GC's subs.

The GC makes money by marking up the subcontractors' costs as a percentage of the construction amount (common) or as a lump sum fee (not so common). For this professional fee, he or she provides the management and scheduling of subs, paying the subs, provides supervision of the construction, provides dumpsters, port-a-john, insurance and other miscellaneous things you need to build a house or construct an addition. The subcontractors make their money by charging for labor and by marking up material.

The GC is the "generalist" and subcontractors are the "specialists." When you need a specific thing fixed in your home, you need a specialist, and that person is the specialty subcontractor, for example, a plumber.

When it comes to hiring someone for maintenance tasks a lot of people who do this work may not be a licensed subcontractor at all. They may just be a "guy with a truck," for example a gutter cleaner, or leaf raker or sometimes a painter. Although using these types of people may work out, you must be careful since workmanship concerns and liability issues still exist but you won't have the legal protection you have when using a licensed contractor. In short, avoid the temptation altogether and always use a licensed contractor.

Deciding When to Use a Contractor

Deciding to use a contractor is one that is often personal. It will come down to evaluating:

• Your comfort level with the task at hand

• Your time

• Your budget

If you're venturing beyond a simple home repair project to new technically challenging installations such as adding electrical circuits or adding a sink, you should first check to see if a permit is required from your local building department. You don't need a permit for many home repairs but you may need a permit for "new work" especially for electrical, heating, cooling and plumbing. In some cases, the permit will require that a licensed contractor does the work to protect the public's health, safety, and welfare. In some cases, it may be required that the local building inspector review your work during construction and after its completion.

If you find that a licensed contractor is not required for the permit or that the work you want to do can be covered under a "Home Owner's Permit" then you should ask yourself three questions:

1. Do I feel confident in making (or at least comfortable trying) this repair?

2. Are the consequences acceptable if it takes me longer to do the project than I anticipate?

3. Do I really want to try this project?

If you answer "no" to any of the above questions, you should probably hire a contractor for the repair. If you answered "yes" to them all, you should give it a shot and repair yourself. That's the only way to gain experience and confidence.

How to Manage the Project

Once you decide to hire a contractor you should know how to effectively manage him, whether it's a quick home repair project or a large home renovation project or new construction. Either way, there are some guidelines to follow in managing the work of anyone you hire to work on your home:

• Hire a licensed, insured contractor.

• Define the expectations of both parties (you and them) and manage to those expectations.

• At a minimum, have a signed document (a contract, or signed and accepted proposal) that outlines what they will do for you (called the Scope of Work), define how much it will cost and where time is an issue define how long it will take and when they will start and finish.

• Define the payment terms before work is started and make the terms part of your signed document.

• Define your expectations and requirements for clean up of their work and protection of surrounding areas as part of the signed document (for example a roofer must protect your landscaping during a roof tear-off and clean up any debris.)

• Discuss the rights of the contractor to access the home when you're not there if required, and the use of your water, electricity. (Note: Try not to have the contractor in your home when you're not there; this protects you and them.)

• Before the contractor starts work, have a friendly conversation about what you want them to be careful with if you have any concerns about things.

• When the work is going on, generally leave the contractor alone. Be friendly but don't get in the way. Casually observe what they are doing. If you are concerned about something you see, ask the contractor about it, but try to let them get their work done. Contractors make their living by getting in and out of a job efficiently.

• Discuss the "extra": The most difficult issue you may experience is the possible request by the contractor for a "Change Order" or "Extra." This results in an added cost to you, which is why you need a clearly defined scope of work. A request for a Change Order is reasonable only if the contractor runs into a situation on the project that was not reasonably anticipated by him, or is a change in scope by you. If you do get a request for a Change Order, review it with the contractor in fairness. If it is a change in scope or resulted in taking more time due to something you did, you should review and pay it if you think it's fair. If it's something that was always part of the scope, you have a more delicate situation and may need to stand firm based on the terms defined in your signed document. Bottom line? If you need to negotiate a price on a Change Order you both did not anticipate, try splitting the difference with him. Rapport and fairness go a long way toward resolving these issues.

• When the repair or maintenance work is complete, make sure you review the work, in person, before you make final payment to the contractor. Make sure the job site is cleaned as expected and the work looks good. Do not be rushed into final payment for any reason.

• If you're happy with their work, tell them.

How to Select a Good Contractor

This may seem daunting but it's pretty straightforward. Try to select contractors you may need on an urgent basis before you need them. Why? Because if you have an emergency repair and need to find someone quickly (who is also good and fair), you don't have time to go through a lengthy selection and screening process. The worst thing you can do is pick someone from the Yellow Pages without interviewing them first.

The easiest and one of the best ways to select a possible contractor is to get references from friends, family or a realtor you trust. Another good method is to use a free service like HomeAdvisor which lets you read real-time reviews of the contractor's work. Once you have some names, meet with them, look for "chemistry" or rapport and observe their level of professionalism. Courtesy, respect, punctuality and the ability to communicate are some of the most important attributes a contractor can have next to their basic competency. No matter how good someone is, if they don't click with you on these points, don't hire them.

You should also be observant for signs of substance abuse such as alcohol or marijuana. If you suspect anything here, do not hire the contractor.

Checklist of things to consider when selecting your contractor.

Use ratings of "Best," "Good," "OK," "Fair" and "Reject" to classify some of these items.

Getting Names of Possible Contractors:

• You have had good personal prior experience working with a contractor [BEST]

• Reliable referral from direct experience of family or friends [GOOD]

• You know of the contractor's reputation but have no direct experience [OK]

• You found them from a trade association or general advertising [FAIR]

State Contractor Licensing (they must provide the number if licensed):

• Licensed; has never had a complaint filed or had disciplinary action taken [BEST]

• Licensed; has no prior complaints filed for at least three or more years [FAIR]

• Licensed; current complaints or actions against them within the past three years [REJECT]

• The contractor has no license [REJECT]

Contractor Insurance (ask to see their certificates):

• Workman's Compensation and General Liability [BEST]

• General Liability only (bodily injury and property damage) [GOOD]

• The contractor has no insurance [REJECT]

Business Longevity:

• In business more than 10 years with the same name [BEST]

• In business five or more years with the same name [GOOD]

• In business one to five years with the same name [OK]

• New business under one year [FAIR]

Stability and Permanence:

• Has a physical business office and address [BEST]

• Has only a Home office or answering service [FAIR]

• Cell phone contact only, no office [REJECT]

Reference Check:

• Positive prior current references from at least five customers [BEST]

• One to four positive references from past customers [FAIR]

• No real references or negative references provided [REJECT]

Experience:

• Specializes in the work you want to be performed [BEST]

• Can perform the work you want but also does other types of work [OK]

• Little to no experience in the work you want to be performed [REJECT]

Scope and Price:

• A detailed description of the scope of work

• Assumptions (if any) are clear and accurate

• Contractor DID NOT offer a discount to "sign up now"

• A contractor will guarantee the work

• All verbal contractor representations are in writing

• No more than 25 to 33 percent asked for upfront

• Final payment not required until work is complete

Getting Bids and Evaluating an Estimate

This is an extremely important aspect of successfully hiring a contractor. Let's break it down:

The Scope of Work:

This defines what the contractor is doing for you. Make sure it covers all the things you want to be completed. It should also spell out any preparation work, protection of surrounding areas, clean up, etc. Reviewing the scope of work between contractors is an essential element of evaluating their bid estimate.

Here are some things to watch for in the scope of different contractors:

• **Painter:** Describe how they plan to prepare the exterior or interior paint surface. This step makes or breaks a paint job. Define if they are hand scraping all loose paint (best), power washing the exterior (be careful as this can damage surrounding areas and you must wait for the wall to fully dry before proceeding with work), priming (best), spot priming (OK). Define the number of coats of paint proposed and the brand and quality of the paint, etc. Make sure they protect surrounding areas and clean up any debris.

• **Landscaper:** No matter what they say or how much they dismiss this issue, make sure they understand you want your shrubs and root balls of your trees planted below the ground. Do not accept making a shallow hole, then placing the plant in it and surrounding the root ball with a mound of dirt and mulch. Make sure they remove the wire around the root ball or untie the twine and place the root ball fully into the ground until only about 6" extends above ground. Make sure they also guarantee the installation and life of the plant for a specified period. Understand your responsibilities for watering.

• **Roofer:** Roofs rarely leak from shingle failure, they leak from flashing failure. What you typically can't see is where water gets in. Make sure they specify where flashing is used. Be concerned and review how they flash an outside corner of a chimney or wall. On a brick home, it's best to cut the brick joints for the flashing and then seal the joint. This is much better than nailing the flashing to the brick wall and relying on caulk. If you live in a cold climate, make sure they install a rubber ice/water shield along the entire edge of your roof extending from the roof's edge to at least 24" past the exterior wall. Make sure they protect your plants and shrubs and clean up any debris daily.

• **Plumber:** If possible, try to negotiate a fixed price for their work. Cleaning out a clogged drain is often priced on a "per foot" basis of the "cleanout snake" used, but some plumbers give a fixed price for this work. Ideally, you should preselect a drain cleaner for emergency drain clean-outs. Bottom line, expect to pay a premium price for emergency calls.

What "Is" and "Is Not" Included in the Bid:

Sometimes a contractor must make allowances or assumptions in their bid, such as material quantity, access to your home, etc. Also, they will sometimes specify what they exclude in the bid. Carefully review assumptions and exclusions with the contractor. Politely question them as to the reasonableness of any assumptions and exclusions. If not, these items will likely become a Change Order later. When you are evaluating and comparing bids between contractors, assumptions and exclusions highlight where you have an apple and an orange.

Contractor Representations:

Your biggest concern here is the contractor's willingness to put in writing any of the verbal representations he or she has made to you to get the job. If they have made oral commitments but won't put them in writing, that's cause for rejection.

Price:

Look for a contract price that is well broken down, clear and easily understood. If it is unclear then they have not taken the time to understand your requirements, the scope of work, or the job. Do not necessarily make your selection only on price.

Incentives:

The contractor mustn't offer you a discount or cash incentives for immediately signing the contract.

Contract Payment Terms:

Ask to be invoiced by mail after the work is completed, but expect most to want payment right after work is done. If they want cash, that's not a great sign. If materials were needed before work can start (e.g., roofer or painter), they want an initial payment for materials. Try to minimize this amount as much as you can. Try not to pay more than 33 percent upfront and only agree to that with a very reputable company.

The Ultimate Home Maintenance Checklist

For many owners, home maintenance happens only when something goes awry. Overflowing gutters, a balky furnace, or a chimney that refuses to draw provoke an expensive emergency call to service technicians. Worse, your family's safety could be in jeopardy when key areas of your home are neglected for too long. To limit or even eliminate service delays, preserve your home's value, and keep everyone comfortable, follow this home maintenance checklist on a regular basis.

Winter

With cold temperatures and harsh elements pressing in, the focus of winter home maintenance is damage control. Because of inclement weather, you may not have the leisure to do extensive exterior repairs.

From a safely secured ladder, check gutters and the lower roof for ice dams and eliminate as necessary.

Check that the covers are still on the outside hose bibs (faucets) and that they have not iced up.

Use this indoor-friendly season as your opportunity to clean the basement, garage, and other interior spaces that get neglected during warm, sunny months.

Keep an eye on your electrical service drop and the line that leads from your home to the power pole (only if you have above-ground electric service). If large branches have fallen on or are hanging on the line, call the electric company for removal.

Make sure that the ground next to the house is graded away from the house to prevent interior flooding.

Spring

Spring home maintenance is chiefly about cleaning up after the mess and damage inflicted by winter.

Clean the gutters and, using a water hose, make sure that they drain.

Check the exterior siding for damage and repair as needed.

When the roof is dry and safe to walk on, check shingles, flashing, and vents for damage.

Clean and replace window screens.

Trim back trees that may deposit branches on your home. For branches near power lines, call your electric company for pruning.

In late spring, install window unit air conditioners.

Reverse ceiling fans so that the vanes rotate in a counter-clockwise direction. This will move air downward, cooling the room.

Summer

With higher temperatures and low precipitation, summer affords comfortable working conditions to make intensive repairs that were not possible in prior seasons.

Make repairs to the home's siding and paint the exterior as needed.

Clean and repair your outside deck.

Wash and apply a sealant to wood fences.

Flush out your water heater to empty it of sediment.

Clean debris from window wells.

Fall

Home maintenance during the fall season is focused on preparing the house for winter.

Test the sump pump by pouring water down the sump pit until the pump turns on.

Remove and store the window screens.

If your home has storm windows, install them.

Remove window unit air conditioners. If you have central air conditioning, winterize it.

Call in a furnace service and have them perform annual maintenance.

Call in a chimney cleaning service or clean the chimney by yourself.

Winterize exterior hose bibs (faucets) by protecting them with foam covers.

Remove leaves and debris from garden ponds and water features.

Reverse ceiling fans so that the vanes rotate in a clockwise direction. This will help distribute the warm air that collects near the ceiling.

Perform regular quarterly maintenance.

Regular Quarterly Maintenance

Every three months, perform these critical maintenance tasks:

Press your smoke detector and carbon monoxide detector buttons to make sure that they are still working. Replace batteries as needed.

Check the gauges on your fire extinguishers to ensure that they are still correctly pressurized.

Check your water heater's temperature and pressure (T&P) valve to make sure that it will expel water. Place a bucket below the relief tube to avoid flooding.

Make sure that your garage door's safety reverse function is working and that the electric eyes are correctly positioned.

For low-use areas such as guest or basement bathrooms, flush the toilet, clean sediment rings from the bowl, and turn on both sink taps.

Check your water softener to make sure that it is topped off with enough salt.

Remove showerheads and sink aerators and soak in vinegar to clean out collected sediment.

Make sure that the dryer vent is properly venting to the outside.

Test all of the GFCI outlets to make sure that they are working properly.

CONCLUSION

When it comes to maintenance and repairs, professional labor can often be one of the more costly parts of a homeowner's budget. While many people will opt to save some cash by doing much of the handiwork themselves, not everyone possesses the skills necessary to fix their own homes—even with the help of instructional online videos. Attempting a DIY project without careful preparation and a complete knowledge of the task at hand could actually result in expenses that far exceed the cost of a contractor. Even if you have the experience and know-how, it's important to consider the time, materials, tools, and permits required for your home improvement project. So, how do you know which projects you can tackle yourself and which you should leave to the experts?

A DIY fix for a drain pipe may be simply tightening a slip-nut near the P-Trap. If the leak is directly from a hole in the drain pipe, a DIY fix would be a flexible coupling with hose clamps. If the leak is from a drain pipe inside the wall, consider calling a professional, says Don Glovan, a franchise consultant with Mr. Rooter Plumbing.

The challenge with hanging wallpaper is getting it straight on the wall and matching up the patterns correctly. It typically requires two people to do the job. Sometimes bubbling can happen, which means a strip of paper will need to be removed and a new strip reinstalled. This can result in not having enough wallpaper and needing to order more. While only you can decide whether the DIY savings outweigh potential risks, hiring a professional guarantees a smooth and predictable outcome, says Tina Nokes, owner of Five Star Painting of Loudoun, VA.

Painting the exterior of a house is a big job. Most homes require all of the trim, soffits, and rake boards and, depending on the type of home, all of the siding as well. This requires extensive use of ladders at high levels and sometimes climbing up on the roof. Homeowners need to consider safety requirements before tackling an exterior job. Five Star Painting recommends hiring a professional with experience and the correct equipment.

A centerset type faucet is a good DIY job—just follow the faucet manufacturer's installation instructions. A more complicated, wide-spread type of faucet with various hose connections on the underside, however, would be best handled by a professional, recommends Glovan.